This Notebook Belongs To:

_____

_____

Gas exchange:

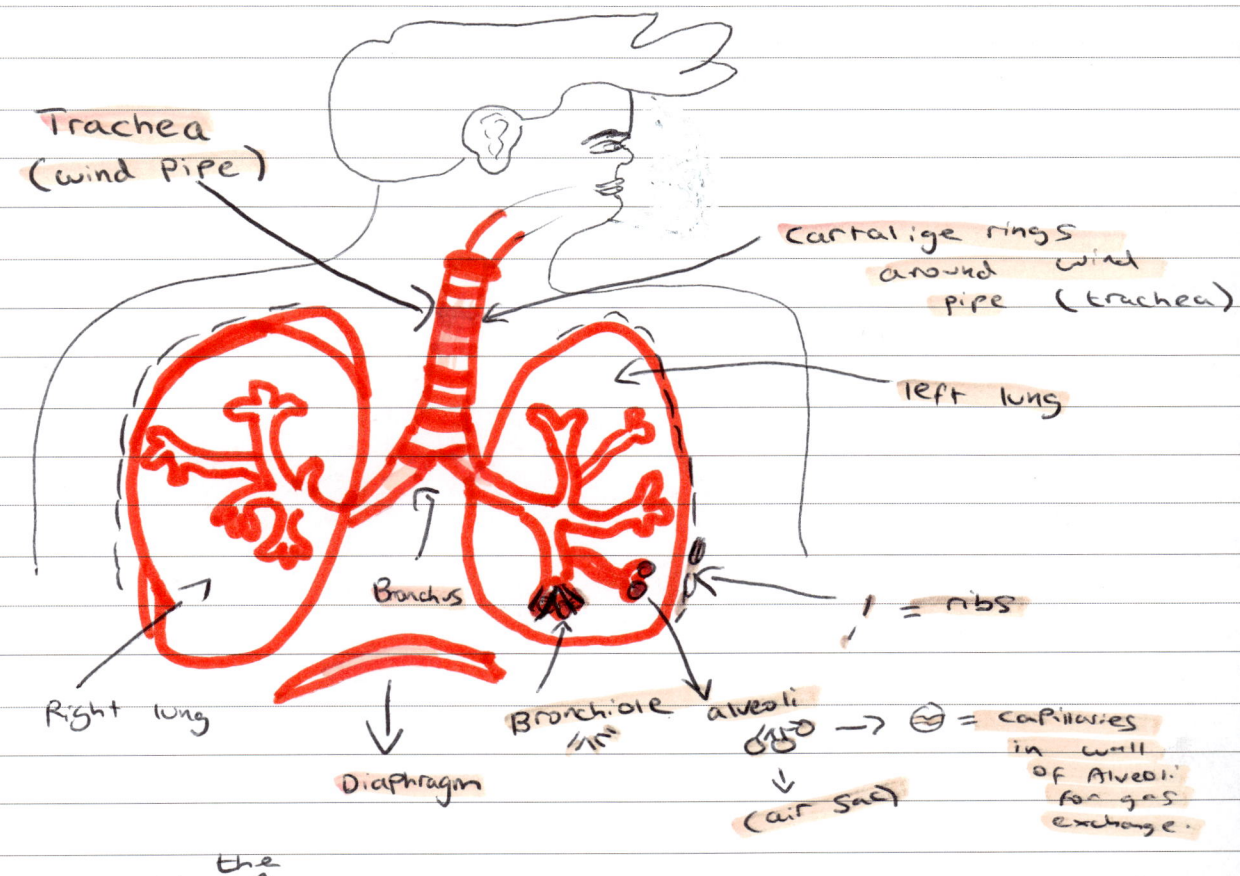

Air enters ~~through~~ the body through the mouth or nose and moves to throat. Then passes through the voice box and enters the Trachea.
↓ (larynx)
(Pharynx)   Strong tube that contains rings of cartalige that prevents it from collapsing.

Within the lungs, the trachea branches into a left and right bronchus. These further divide into smaller and smaller branches called bronchioles.
The smallest bronchioles end in tiny air sacs. These are called alveoli.
↓
They inflate when a person inhales and deflate when a person exhales.

During gas exchange Oxygen moves from the lungs to the bloodstream. At the same time Carbon dioxide passes from the blood to the lungs. This happens in the lungs between the alveoli and capillaries, which are located in the walls of the alveoli. Oxygen molecules attach to red blood cells, which travel back to the heart. At the same time, the carbon dioxide molecules in the alveoli are blown out of the body the next time a person exhales. Gas exchange allows the body to replenish the oxygen and eliminate the carbon dioxide to survive.

How does a large surface area affect gas exchange?

Having a large surface area increases the amount of gas that can diffuse into and out of the lungs.
The greater the surface area, the more gas exchange can occur.

How and where does gas exchange occur in humans?

Gas exchange occurs in the alveoli and blood in the capillaries that supply the lungs for humans.

Oxygen moves from the lungs into the bloodstream. At the same time carbon dioxide passes from the blood to the lungs.
Your lungs get rid of the 'waste' (carbon dioxide) when you exhale.

Blood vessels:
1. Capillaries - tiny + thin blood vessels
2. Veins - Takes blood towards the heart. Deoxygenated blood.
3. Arteries - takes blood away from the heart. Oxygenated blood.

Oxygen molecules attach to red blood cells, which travel back to the heart.

The Anatomy of the Heart

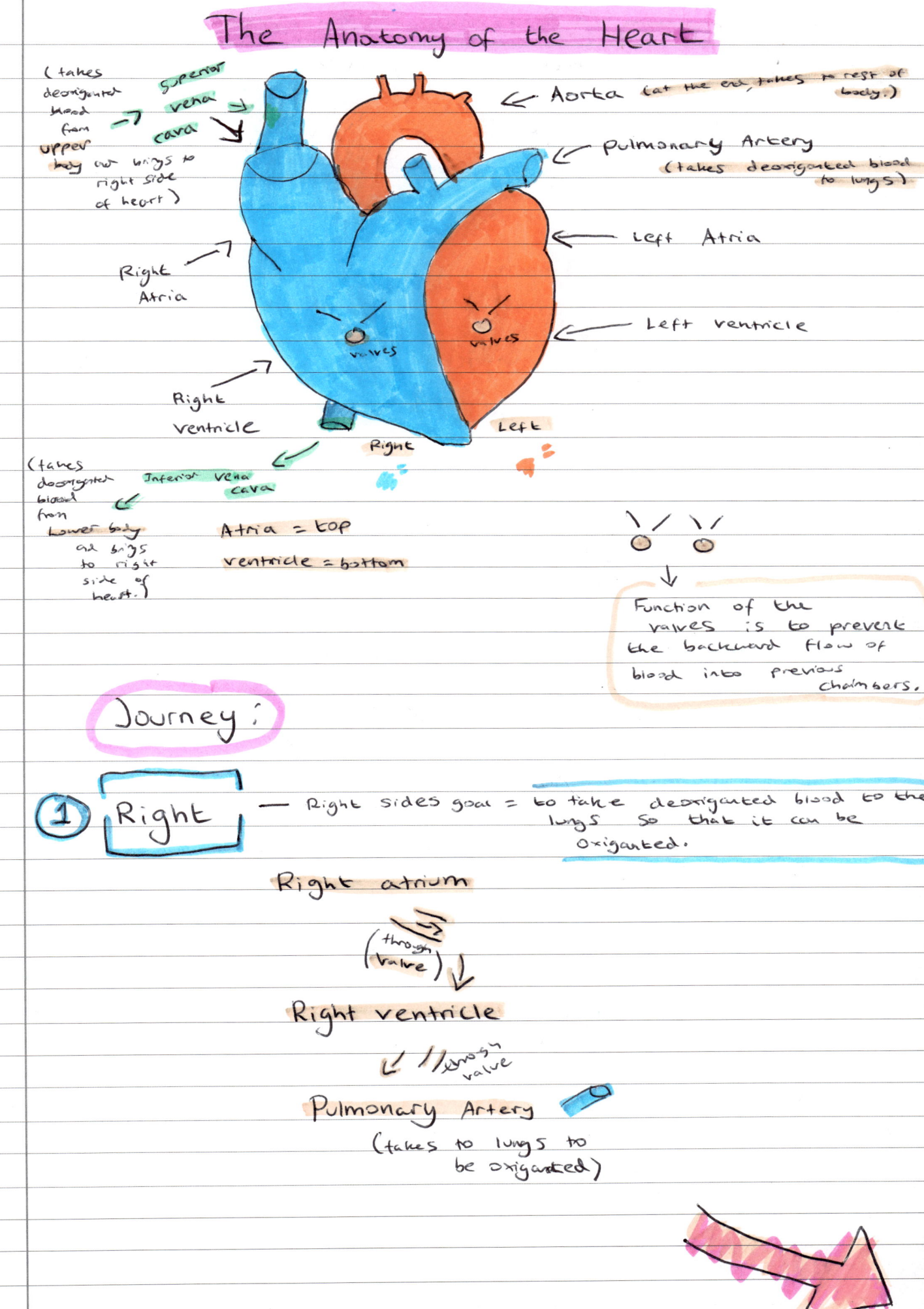

(takes deoxigenated blood from upper body and brings to right side of heart) → superior vena cava

Aorta (at the end, takes to rest of body)

Pulmonary Artery (takes deoxigenated blood to lungs)

Left Atria

Right Atria

Left ventricle

Right ventricle

(takes deoxigenated blood from lower body and brings to right side of heart) → Inferior vena cava

Atria = top
ventricle = bottom

Function of the valves is to prevent the backward flow of blood into previous chambers.

Journey:

① **Right** — Right sides goal = to take deoxigenated blood to the lungs so that it can be oxigenated.

Right atrium
↓ (through valve)
Right ventricle
↓ through valve
Pulmonary Artery
(takes to lungs to be oxigenated)

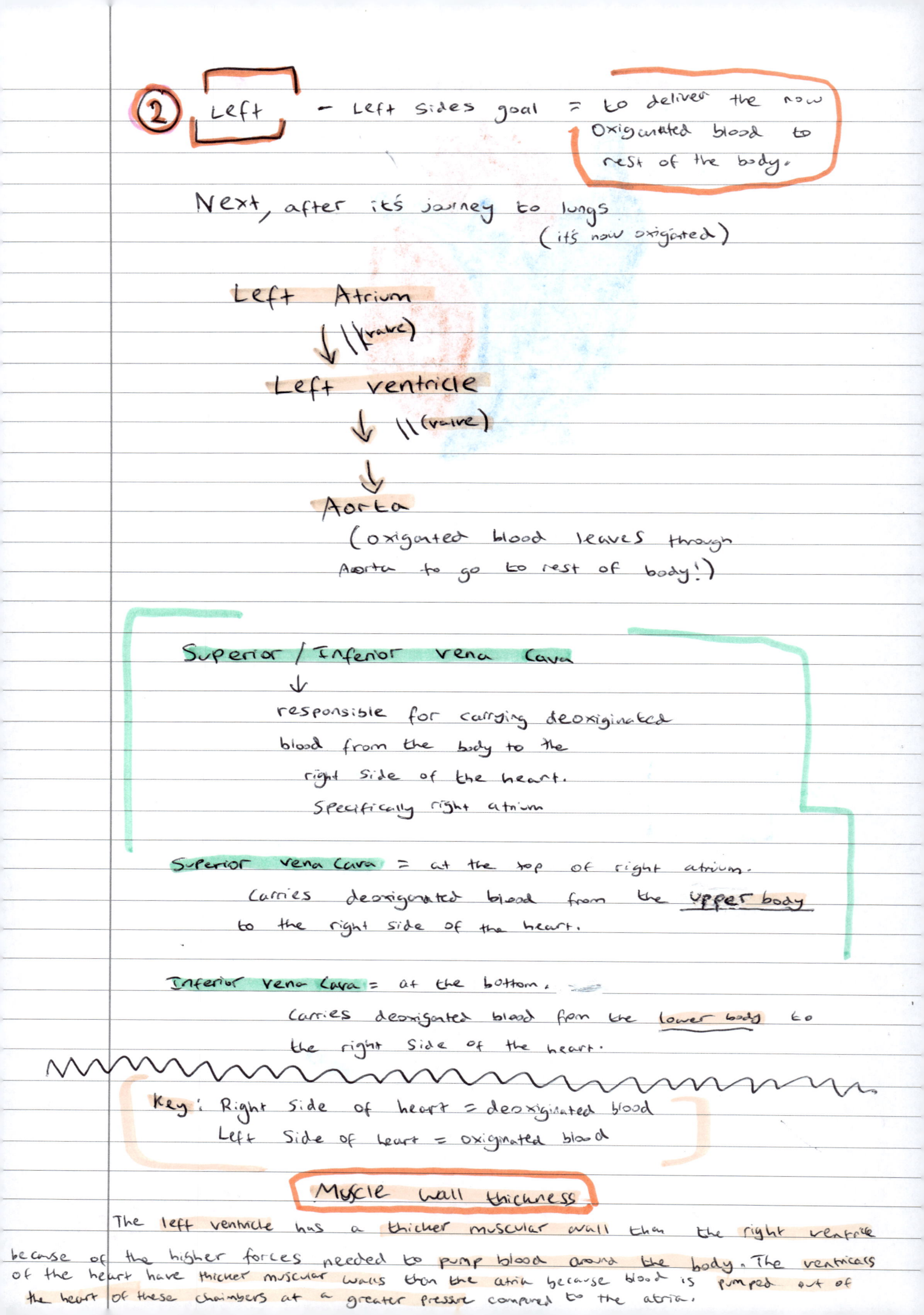

② **Left** — Left sides goal = to deliver the now oxigenated blood to rest of the body.

Next, after it's journey to lungs
(it's now oxigenated)

Left Atrium
↓ (valve)
Left ventricle
↓ (valve)
↓
Aorta
(oxigenated blood leaves through Aorta to go to rest of body!)

Superior / Inferior vena Cava
↓
responsible for carrying deoxiginated blood from the body to the right side of the heart.
Specifically right atrium

Superior vena Cava = at the top of right atrium. Carries deoxiginated blood from the <u>upper body</u> to the right side of the heart.

Inferior vena Cava = at the bottom. Carries deoxiginated blood from the <u>lower body</u> to the right side of the heart.

~~~~~~

Key: Right side of heart = deoxiginated blood
Left side of heart = oxiginated blood

Muscle wall thickness

The left ventricle has a thicker muscular wall than the right ventricle because of the higher forces needed to pump blood around the body. The ventricles of the heart have thicker muscular walls than the atria because blood is pumped out of the heart of these chambers at a greater pressure compared to the atria.

Inspired and expired air

Inspired air — The air that we breathe in (inhale)
Expired air — The air that we breathe out (exhale)

Limewater is used as it can be used to detect carbon dioxide.
↓
If carbon dioxide is bubbled through limewater then it turns from clear to cloudy/milky in colour. This is why limewater can be used to test for carbon dioxide.

[More carbon dioxide is present in expired air (exhaled) compared to inspired air (inhaled).]

(Differences)

Inspired air | **Expired air**
↓ — Variable temp | ↓
- Lots of Oxygen (as we breathe it in) | - Lots of carbon dioxide (as we breathe it out)
- Contains less water vapour | - Contains more water vapour
 | - Body's temp

Key:
Variable = factor that CAN be changed
Independent variable = variable that doesn't change

The affects of physical activity on the rate and depth of breathing

When you excersise, your muscles work harder, your body uses more oxygen and produces more carbon dioxide. To cope with this extra demand, your breathing has to increase. So, the rate and depth of breathing increases due to the ~~heart rate~~ heart rate increasing, this makes sure that oxygen is absorbed into the blood, and more carbon dioxide is removed from it.

The importance of the Septum in Seperating Oxyginated and Deoxiginated Blood.

The Septum helps keep oxyginated blood from the lungs, from mixing with deoxiginated blood from the body. It does this by seperating the atria and ventricles so it forms a barrier between the heart chambers and prevents mixing oxyginated and deoxygated blood.

The Septum (in heart not nose) is located between the right and left ventricles of the heart.

Functioning of the heart in terms of the contraction of muscles of the atria and ventricles + the action of the valves.

For the heart to keep pumping, electrical signals are sent to the heart muscle telling it when to contract and relax.

As the heart muscles contract and relax, the valves open and shut. This let's blood flow into the ventricles and atria at alternate times.

Structure of Arteries and veins.

Arteries and veins link your heart to the rest of the Circulatory System. Veins bring blood to your heart. Arteries take blood away from your heart.
Valves control the direction of the blood flow.

The walls of the veins have the same three layers as the arteries, although there is less smooth muscle and connective tissue. The walls of the veins are thinner than those of the arteries, because blood in the veins has less pressure than in the arteries.

Coronary heart disease

Coronary heart disease is when your coronary arteries become narrowed by a build up of fatty material within their walls.

Coronary arteries supply your heart with oxygenated blood.

Risks/causes of Coronary heart disease:

- overweight
- not physically active
- unhealthy eating
- smoking tobacco
- family history of CHD
- stress

→ also family history of the disease at a early age (50 or younger.)

The main treatments for Coronary heart disease are healthy lifestyle changes and medicine. Some people may need surgery.

To reduce the risk of getting it you can be more active and make sure your diet is healthy.

Having a healthy weight reduces your chances of developing high blood pressure. High blood pressure causes a strain and causes the coronary arteries to become narrowed from plaque or other substances. Regular exercise will also keep your blood pressure at a healthy level and will make your heart and blood circulatory system more efficient.

Blood vessels

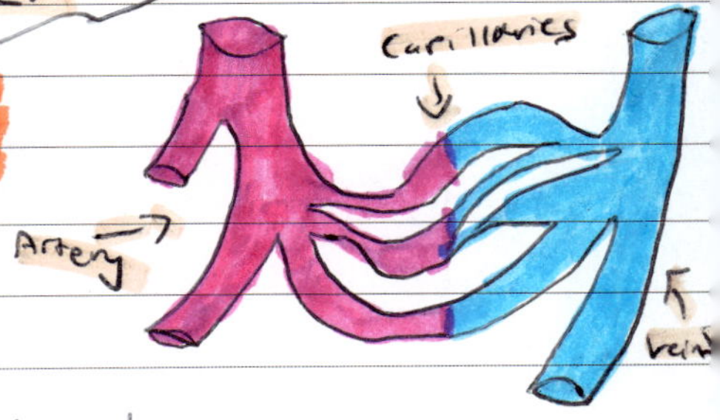

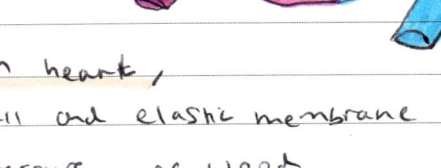

There are 3 blood vessels

① Arteries - carry blood away from heart, has thick muscle wall and elastic membrane to handle with high pressure of blood

② veins - carry blood back to heart.

③ Capillaries - They have a very thin wall to enable diffusion. Where oxygen and nutrients are exchanged for carbon dioxide and waste.

The role of Hemoglobin

Haemoglobin is found in red blood cells. It's function is transporting oxygen in the blood.

Hormones

FSH
Follicle stimulating hormone

- A hormone made in the pituitary gland, it acts on the ovaries to make the follicles of eggs grow.

Printed in Great Britain
by Amazon